RAF, Dominion & Allied S[quadrons] AT WAR:

Study, History and Statistics

COMPILED BY
Phil H. Listemann

Drawings by Claveworks Classics

PREFACE

The purpose of this study is to provide aviation historians and enthusiasts with a range of information relative to each of the Commonwealth squadrons that saw combat during World War II. Each record will comprise a short history, complete with illustrations and artwork, and accompanied by the following appendices:

Appendix I: Squadron Commanders and Flight Commanders
Appendix II: Major awards
Appendix III: Operational diary (number of sorties per month)
Appendix IV: Victory list
Appendix V: Aircraft losses on operations
Appendix VI: Aircraft losses in accidents
Appendix VII: Aircraft Serial numbers matching with individual letters (including mission totals for multi-engine aircraft)
Appendix VIII: Nominal roll (Captains only for bomber and seaplane units)
Appendix IX: Roll of Honour

Individual files will be constantly updated, when any fresh information comes to light. Additional information will be available for download, at no charge, on each squadron's site at:

GLOSSARY OF TERMS

RANKS

AC: Aircraftman
G/C: Group Captain
W/C: Wing Commander
S/L: Squadron Leader
F/L: Flight Lieutenant
F/O: Flying Officer
P/O: Pilot Officer
W/O: Warrant Officer
F/Sgt: Flight Sergeant
Sgt: Sergeant
Cpl: Corporal
LAC: Leading Aircraftman

OTHER

AAF: Auxiliary Air Force
CO: Commanding Officer
DFC: Distinguished Flying Cross

DFM: Distinguished Flying Medal
DSO: Distinguished Service Order
Eva.: Evaded
Inj.: Injured
ORB: Operational Record Book
OTU: Operational Training Unit
PAF: Polish Air Force
PoW: Prisoner of War
RAF: Royal Air Force
RAAF: Royal Australian Air Force
RCAF: Royal Canadian Air Force
RNZAF: Royal New Zealand Air Force
SAAF: South African Air Force
Sqn: Squadron
TOC: Taken on charge
†: Killed

No. 313 (Czechoslovakian) Squadron 1941-1945

ISBN: 978-2918590-75-0

Contributors & Acknowledgments:
Tomas Polak, Jiri Rajlich, Andrew Thomas, Pavel Vancata

Cover: Side view of AR549/RY-E during the summer of 1942. This Spitfire Mk. V served over a year with 313 before being passed on to the Polish 317 Squadron.

Main Equipment

Spitfire I	Mar.41 - Aug.41
Spitfire II	Aug.41 - Nov.41
Spitfire V	Oct.41 - Feb.44
Spitfire VI	Jun.43 - Jul.43
Spitfire VII	Feb.44 - Jul.44
Spitfire IX	Feb.44 - Jul.44
	Oct.44 - Feb.46

Squadron Code Letters:

RY

Squadron History

No. 313 (Czechoslovakian) Squadron was the third Czech-manned fighter squadron in the RAF. It was officially formed on **10 May 1941** at Catterick. This formation had been dictated more by political considerations than military. Indeed, since the formation of the first Czech squadrons in the RAF the previous year, the Czechs and the RAF knew that the small reserve of flying personnel, and lack of ground crew, would lead to critical problems in maintaining these squadrons at an operational status. However the Czech government in exile insisted on forming a third fighter squadron so that a wing unit could be formed and give greater political impact abroad. Despite this short reserve, the British finally agreed to provide the extra personnel, especially ground crew, required. Within a month the squadron became operational but was restricted to convoy patrols at first. The squadron was progressively engaged in more offensive tasks and its peak of activity took place in the summer of 1942 alongside the other two Czech fighter squadrons. Its pilots claimed 13 of the 17 aircraft claimed as destroyed or probably destroyed that year but the squadron sustained heavy losses at the same time and, by 1943, was less engaged and generally inactive for a short period of time. What the RAF feared eventually happened in 1943 when a shortage of replacement pilots, for those who had been killed or rested, led to the arrival of many Commonwealth pilots, from the summer of 1943, to fill the gap and maintain 313 as an operational squadron. The Czech reserves were really only enough for the first two Czech fighter units. The situation was made worse when many Czech pilots resigned from the RAF in February 1944 to fight alongside the Soviets who had also formed a Czech fighter unit. More Commonwealth pilots were therefore posted in. The last major action 313 (with the rest of the Czech Wing) was involved in was the D-Day landings but, here, their participation ceased after two weeks as the RAF expected heavy losses for 2 TAF units in the weeks to come over Normandy. The squadron was sent to Scotland and returned to the fight in an escort role from the British Isles. This limited the risk of heavy losses. With the two other Czech squadrons, 313 returned to Czechoslovakia in August 1945 and was disbanded on **15 February 1946**.

Squadron Bases

Catterick	10.05.41 - 01.07.41	Ibsley	20.01.44 - 20.02.44
Leconsfield	01.07.41 - 26.08.41	Mendlesham	20.02.44 - 14.03.44
Portreath	26.08.41 - 23.11.41	Southend	14.03.44 - 20.03.44
Warmwell	23.11.41 - 29.11.41	Mendlesham	20.03.44 - 04.04.44
Portreath	29.11.41 - 15.12.41	Appledram	04.04.44 - 22.06.44
Hornchurch	15.12.41 - 06.02.42	Tangmere	22.06.44 - 28.06.44
Southend	06.02.42 - 07.03.42	B.10/Plumetot (France)	28.06.44 - 29.06.44
Hornchurch	07.03.42 - 29.04.42	Tangmere	29.06.44 - 04.07.44
Fairlop	29.04.42 - 08.06.42	Lympne	04.07.44 - 11.07.44
Church Stanton	08.06.42 - 28.06.43	Skaebrae	11.07.44 - 04.10.44
Peterhead	28.06.43 - 21.08.43	North Weald	04.10.44 - 29.12.44
Hawkinge	21.08.43 - 18.09.43	Bradwell Bay	29.12.44 - 27.02.45
Ibsley	18.09.43 - 06.01.44	Manston	27.02.45 - 07.08.45
Woodvale	06.01.44 - 10.01.44	Hildesheim (Germany)	07.08.45 - 13.08.45
Ayr	10.01.44 - 20.01.44	Prague (Czechoslovakia)	13.08.45 - 15.02.46

WHAT THEY DID BEFORE JOINING THE RAF

When World War II broke out in September 1939, Czechoslovakia had already ceased to exist. The country which had been created at the end of WWI from former Austro-Hungarian territories had built up strong armed forces in the years between the wars. It also had a competitive aeronautical industry which allowed it to be almost self-sufficient. By the time of the Munich Crisis the Czechoslovakian Air Force (CzAF) consisted of six Air Regiments, one fighter (4th), three mixed fighter/reconnaissance (1st, 2nd, 3rd), and two bombers (5th and 6th). A total of more than 1,500 aircraft, about 830 of them being first-line types including more than 320 fighters were available to the Allied cause. Its pilots and aircrew were well trained and motivated. After September 1938 when French and Britsih politicians sold out to Germany, this Air Force was gradually disbanded. The final chapter in Czechoslovakia's short history took place in March 1939 when the country was split into two parts. Bohemia-Moravia which was made a German protectorate, and Slovakia, officially independent from the Germans, but with strong political and military links.

Soldiers, pilots and other aircrew were demobilised and many chose to escape from their country and find asylum in Poland, where some remained, or France, the preferred choice for most of them. By September 1939 nearly 500 of them had joined the French forces, serving at first in the French Foreign Legion for diplomatic reasons as France and Germany were not yet at war. With the oubreak of war the French were happy to find additional well-trained pilots in their midst and they were transferred to the *Armée de l'Air* (French Air Force - FAF) in October 1939. The first pilots were ready for active service as early as December 1939 but were scattered throughout French fighter units (*Groupe de Chasse* - GC), though a few found their way to bomber or reconnaissance units. As other Czechoslovak airmen arrived they were sent to the Czech Depot at Agde near the Mediterranean coast for future allocation to units. Plans to create separate Czechoslovakian units were in hand but these did not come to fruition. Nevertheless the Czechs performed well, and were much appreciated by the French. About 157 confirmed or probable victories were claimed by Czechoslovak pilots, although a number of these would have been classified as "shared" under the British system of calculating kills. Some pilots like Alois Vasatko, with 15 victories, and Frantisek Perina with 14 were amongst the top aces in the French Air Force during the Phoney war and the battle of France. These scores were not achieved without cost, 28 airmen were killed while serving with the French. With the end of the Battle of France, the Czechoslovaks withdrew to Great Britain, the last European country still fighting against Nazi Germany. The Czechoslovaks had not yet been defeated. By 15th August 1940 more than 900 former CzAF personnel had reached Great Britain and this total rose to nearly 1,300 by the end of 1940. These men were the the nucleus of four Czech units, Nos.310, 312 and 313 fighter Squadrons, and No.311 bomber Squadron. One night fighter flight was raised as part of No.68 Squadron.

They were to fight well for a foreign King and country and some, at least, survived to return to their own liberated country.

Czech front-line pilots killed serving with the French

Sgt Josef BENDL	†07.06.40	GC I/6	Sgt Josef KOSNAR	†05.06.40	GC III/7
Lt Jindrich BERAN (1)	†12.05.40	GC III/3	Sgt Jan KRAKORA	†23.04.40	GC I/1
Lt Frantisek BIEBERLE (1)	†25.05.40	GC I/6	Lt Jiri KRAL (1)	†08.06.40	GC I/1
S/Lt Josef DEKASTELLO (1)	†03.06.40	GC I/8	Sgt Antonin KRALIK (1)	†27.05.40	GC I/8
Lt Frantisek DYMA	†21.05.40	GC III/7	Lt Antonin MIKOLASEK (2)	†25.05.40	GC II/3
Lt Jaroslav GLEICH (2)	†13.06.40	GC II/3	S/Chef Emil MORAVEK	†15.06.40	GC I/5
Cap Timoteus HAMSIK (1)	†14.05.40	GC I/5	S/Chef Josef NOVAK	†02.06.40	GC III/3
Adj Josef HRANICKA (1)	†03.06.40	GC I/6	Sgt Stanislav POPELKA (1)	†03.06.40	GC I/6
Lt Otakar KOREC	†05.06.40	GC I/3	Sgt Vladimir VASEK	†02.01.40	GC I/5

Furthermore, other Czech airmen were killed, at CIC (*Centre d'Instruction à la Chasse* - Fighter OTU) :
Sol. Frantisek BARTON (06.10.39), Lt Vladimir KUCERA (14.05.40), Sgt Miloslav RAJTR (11.01.40)
or at CIB (*Centre d'Instruction au Bombardement* - Bomber OTU) :
Sol. Jaroslav KRIZEK (15.11.39), Cap Jaroslav Novak (15.12.39) and Cpl Jaroslav STOKLASA (04.03.40) or for other causes, Capt Frantisek NOVAK [2](27.04.40, illness), Capt Jan CERNY (11.05.40, air raid), and Sgt Frantisek MASEK (18.06.40, bomber pilot, accident), as well Cpl Zdenech EICHELMAN, mechanic (29.04.40).

In brackets, the number of victories claimed with the French.

From left to right, the prewar Czechoslovak Air Force's Regiment's badges, 1st to 6th.

APPENDIX I
Squadron and Flight Commanders

Rank and Name	SN	Origin	Dates
S/L Gordon L. Sinclair	RAF No.39644	RAF	10.05.41 - 24.09.41
S/L Josef Jaske	RAF No.83226	(cz)/RAF	24.09.41 - 15.12.41
S/L Karel Mrazek	RAF No.82561	(cz)/RAF	15.12.41 - 24.06.42
S/L Jaroslav Himr	RAF No.81891	(cz)/RAF	24.06.42 - 24.09.43
S/L Frantisek Fajtl	RAF No.82544	(cz)/RAF	24.09.43 - 31.01.44
S/L Vaclav Bergman	RAF No.81884	(cz)/RAF	31.01.44 - 22.05.44
S/L Alois Hochmal	RAF No.82548	(cz)/RAF	22.05.44 - 01.09.44
S/L Karel Kasal	RAF No.81893	(cz)/RAF	01.09.44 - 15.11.44
S/L Otmar L. Kucera	RAF No.112548	(cz)/RAF	15.11.44 - 13.08.45

A Flight

Rank and Name	SN	Origin	Dates
F/L Karel Mrazek	RAF No.82561	(cz)/RAF	17.05.41 - 04.06.41
F/L John L. Kilmartin	RAF No.39793	RAF	04.06.41 - 25.06.41
F/L Karel Mrazek	RAF No.82561	(cz)/RAF	25.06.41 - 15.12.41
F/L Frantisek Fajtl	RAF No.82544	(cz)/RAF	15.12.41 - 27.04.42
F/L Frantisek Vancl	RAF No.87628	(cz)/RAF	27.04.42 - 21.05.42
F/L Vaclav Hajek	RAF No.87617	(cz)/RAF	21.05.42 - 01.10.42
F/L Jaroslav Muzika	RAF No.82562	(cz)/RAF	01.10.42 - 07.08.43
F/L Alois Hochmal	RAF No.82548	(cz)/RAF	07.08.43 - 21.05.44
F/L Vaclav Slouf	RAF No.112547	(cz)/RAF	21.05.44 - 30.09.44
F/L Frantisek Masarik	RAF No.120196	(cz)/RAF	30.09.44 - 13.08.45

B Flight

Rank and Name	SN	Origin	Dates
F/L Jan Cermak	RAF No.84666	(cz)/RAF	19.05.41 - 03.06.41
F/L Thomas W. Gillen	RAF No.70245	RAF	03.06.41 - 15.09.41
F/L Stanislav Fejfar	RAF No.82545	(cz)/RAF	15.09.41 - 20.03.42
F/L Karel Vykoukal	RAF No.82545	(cz)/RAF	20.03.42 - 13.04.42
F/L Stanislav Fejfar	RAF No.82545	(cz)/RAF	13.04.42 - 17.05.42
F/L Vaclav Raba	RAF No.82569	(cz)/RAF	17.05.42 - 01.10.42
F/L Bohuslav Kimlicka	RAF No.82553	(cz)/RAF	01.10.42 - 01.01.43
F/L Vaclav Bergman	RAF No.81884	(cz)/RAF	01.01.43 - 01.09.43
F/L Otmar L. Kucera	RAF No.112548	(cz)/RAF	01.09.43 - 01.05.44
F/L Ronald Wood	RAF No.121525	RAF	01.05.44 - 28.02.45
F/L Karel Zouhar	RAF No.130858	(cz)/RAF	28.02.45 - 13.08.45

APPENDIX II
MAJOR AWARDS

DSO: -

DFC: 4

Vaclav **Jicha** (RAF No.66486), *CZECHOSLOVAKIA*
Otmar Leopold **Kucera** (RAF No.112548), *CZECHOSLOVAKIA*
Karel **Mrazek** (RAF No.82561), *CZECHOSLOVAKIA*
Josef **Prihoda** (RAF No.110307), *CZECHOSLOVAKIA*

DFM: -

APPENDIX III
OPERATIONAL DIARY
NUMBER OF SORTIES PER MONTH

Date	Month	Total	Date	Month	Total
Jun.41	71	71	Sep.43	301	5,937
Jul.41	125	196	Oct.43	144	6,081
Aug.41	202	398	Nov.43	145	6,226
Sep.41	189	587	Dec.43	146	6,372
Oct.41	237	824	Jan.44	32	6,404
Nov.41	166	990	Feb.44	115	6,519
Dec.41	109	1,099	Mar.44	81	6,600
Jan.42	98	1,197	Apr.44	129	6,729
Feb.42	161	1,358	May.44	380	7,109
Mar.42	224	1,582	Jun.44	640	7,749
Apr.42	386	1,968	Jul.44	138	7,887
May.42	292	2,260	Aug.44	128	8,015
Jun.42	288	2,548	Sep.44	125	8,140
Jul.42	293	2,841	Oct.44	96	8,236
Aug.42	347	3,188	Nov.44	125	8,361
Sep.42	241	3,429	Dec.44	90	8,451
Oct.42	164	3,593	Jan.45	29	8,480
Nov.42	162	3,755	Feb.45	135	8,615
Dec.42	85	3,840	Mar.219	219	8,834
Jan.43	132	3,972	Apr.45	120	8,954
Feb.43	230	4,202	May.45	16	8,970
Mar.43	222	4,424			
Apr.43	360	4,784			
May.43	319	5,103	**Grand Total**		**8,970**
Jun.43	247	5,350			
Jul.43	160	5,510			
Aug.43	126	5,636			

Extracted from AIR27/1697-1698

APPENDIX IV
VICTORY LIST
CONFIRMED (C) AND PROBABLE (P) CLAIMS

Date	Pilot	SN	Origin	Type	Serial	Code	Nb	Cat.

SPITFIRE V

Date	Pilot	SN	Origin	Type	Serial	Code	Nb	Cat.
28.03.42	P/O Vaclav JICHA	RAF No.66486	(CZ)/RAF	Fw190	BL769	RY-E	1.0	C
	S/L Karel MRAZEK	RAF No.82561	(CZ)/RAF	Bf109	P8531	RY-R	1.0	C
	Sgt Jiri REZNICEK	RAF No.787691	(CZ)/RAF	Bf109	AD390	RY-L	1.0	P
	F/O Frantisek VANCL	RAF No.87628	(CZ)/RAF	Bf109	AB276	RY-K	1.0	P
10.04.42	F/Sgt Vaclav FOGLAR	RAF No.787662	(CZ)/RAF	Bf109	P8571	RY-R	1.0	C
	F/L Vaclav HAJEK	RAF No.87617	(CZ)/RAF	Bf109	AB276	RY-K	1.0	P
12.04.42	F/L Frantisek FAJTL	RAF No.82544	(CZ)/RAF	Bf109	BM127	RY-F	0.5	C
	Sgt Prokop BRAZDA	RAF No.787673	(CZ)/RAF		W3177	RY-G	0.5	C
27.04.42	P/O Josef PRIHODA	RAF No.110307	(CZ)/RAF	Fw190	BM301	RY-R	1.0	C
30.04.42	Sgt Jaroslav HLOUZEK	RAF No.787338	(CZ)/RAF	Bf109	AA765	RY-V	1.0	C
05.05.42	F/L Stanislav FEJFAR	RAF No.82545	(CZ)/RAF	Fw190	BL973	RY-S	1.0	C
				Fw190	BL973	RY-S	1.0	P
	P/O Otmar L. KUCERA	RAF No.112548	(CZ)/RAF	Fw190	BM323	RY-P	1.0	C
23.06.42	P/O Josef PRIHODA	RAF No.110307	(CZ)/RAF	Fw190	BM295		1.0	C
27.08.43	S/L Jaroslav HIMR	RAF No.81891	(CZ)/RAF	Fw190	AB918		1.0	C
24.09.43	S/L Jaroslav HIMR	RAF No.81891	(CZ)/RAF	Bf110	BP826		1.0	C
	F/Sgt Alois ZALESKY	RAF No.787439	(CZ)/RAF	Bf110	AD427		1.0	C
27.09.43	F/L Otmar L. KUCERA	RAF No.112548	(CZ)/RAF	Fw190	EE659	RY-V	1.0	C

SPITFIRE IX

Date	Pilot	SN	Origin	Type	Serial	Code	Nb	Cat.
09.07.44	Sgt Karel STOJAR	RAF No.654725	(CZ)/RAF	V-1	ML145		1.0	C

Total: 17.0

Aircraft damaged: 17.5

APPENDIX V
AIRCRAFT LOST ON OPERATIONS

Date	Pilot	S/N	Origin	Serial	Code	Mark	Fate

SPITFIRE

Date	Pilot	S/N	Origin	Serial	Code	Mark	Fate
01.12.41	F/O Karel VYKOUKAL	RAF No.81902	(CZ)/RAF	W3962	RY-X	VB	-

At 12.05, F/O Vykoukal took off with Sgt Cap for a convoy patrol when he encountered engine trouble and was obliged to make a forced landing near Boscawen Rose Farm. He escaped unhurt. The aircraft was first thought to be repairable but it was eventually re-categorised E a couple of weeks later. Vykoukal was a pre-war Czechoslovak Air Force pilot serving with Air Regiment 4. He escaped to France in October 1939 and joined the Armée de l´Air. After the fall of France he fled to the United Kingdom and enlisted in the RAF and was posted to No. 310 (Czech) Squadron in July on its formation but in August he was posted to No. 6 OTU for further training and then posted to No. 111 Squadron in September before a further transfer to No 73 Squadron two weeks later. In November he went to No. 151 Squadron and in December 1940 he was posted to No. 17 Squadron before joining

313 in May 1941. In April 1942, he was posted to No. 41 Squadron as a flight commander but failed to return from a Shipping Recce sortie on 25 May 1942.

Note on the aircraft: TOC 14.10.41. Issued 313 (Czech) Sqn 23.10.41.

11.01.42   Sgt Josef **VALENTA**   RAF No.787681   (CZ)/RAF   **AD424**   RY-S   VB   †

Four aircraft of the squadron took off at 09.50 on 11 January for a convoy patrol. Valenta was delayed on take off for about 10 minutes. When he finally get airborne the weather was so bad that he decided to land. He turned back and the ground staff saw him pass the hangars at about 230 feet. Turning again, his Spitfire lost speed and crashed into a field, near the anti-aircraft gun positions, adjoining the southern perimeter of the airfield. This happened at 10.05 am. Valenta was a pre-war Czechoslovak Air Force man who didn't complete his training, having enlisted in April 1938. After establishment of the Protectorate Böhmen und Mähren, in March 1939, he escaped to France. In October 1939 he enlisted in the Armée de l´Air and then trained as a fighter pilot but did not reach operational status. After the fall of France he was evacuated to the United Kingdom to join the RAF. On completion of his training, he was posted, in April 1941, to No. 56 Squadron and in June transferred to 313. After one month he was transferred to No. 452 Squadron (RAAF) but changed to No. 72 Squadron before returning to 313 in August 1941.

Note on the aircraft: TOC 19.10.41. Issued 313 (Czech) Sqn date non recorded.

23.02.42   Sgt Frantisek **BÖNISH**   RAF No.788038   (CZ)/RAF   **AD391**   RY-H   VB   †

Led by F/L Fajtl, four Spitfires took off at 09.55 for a convoy patrol over the Thames estuary to be flown at 750/1,000 feet. Visibility was one mile and cloud 10/10. At 10.36 witnesses saw a Spitfire diving from 1,500 feet. The starboard wing touched the water first and, after bouncing twice, the machine went straight into the water six miles south-east of Southend between Southend and Shoeburyness. Bönish's body was recovered twenty minutes later and found to have suffered a fatal skull fracture. It is believed, with the poor visibility, Bönish misjudged the true height of his aircraft. Frantisek Bönish was a pre-war Czecho-slovakian pilot who had escaped his country via Poland, joined the Polish Air Force and fell into Soviet hands on 18 September 1939. Released from captivity in 1941 he joined the RAF and retrained. He had joined the squadron in August 1941.

Note on the aircraft: TOC 13.10.41. Issued to No. 313 Sqn on 26.10.41.

18.03.42   Sgt Miroslav **ZAUF**   RAF No.787496   (CZ)/RAF   **AA869**   VB   †

Sgt Zauf (Yellow 2) took off at 15.20 as wingman to Sgt Špaček (Yellow 1) for a Rhubarb sortie south-east of Condette. The target was the railways between Boulogne and Le Touquet (France). The weather was bad, with a cloud layer of 9/10, a base at 1,500 feet with visibility of four miles. The English coast was crossed at zero feet at Dungeness. Fifty German soldiers were seen drilling in front of a factory and the two pilots made three separate attacks. However, contact was lost by Yellow 1 and Sgt Špaček returned to base alone and landed at 16.15. Špaček tried to contact his wingman on the radio-transmitter without success. Miroslav Zauf had served with the squadron since September 1941 but his background is not known.

Note on the aircraft: TOC 20.10.41, to 313 Sqn four days later.

27.03.42   P/O Vladimir **MICHÁLEK**   RAF No.68727   (CZ)/RAF   **AD197**   VB   †

In the afternoon, the Hornchurch Wing (616, 313, 411 Squadrons) took off at 14.30 to escort bombers attacking Ostend. The wing was led by W/C Powell while 313 was led by S/L Hrabák. The squadron was flying at 12,000 feet. In the vicinity of Ostend the squa-dron was attacked by German fighters and after a few seconds Michálek's Spitfire was seen to spin into the sea. His victor was Hauptmann Josef 'Pips' Priller of JG 26. Vladimir Michálek fled his country when it passed under full German control and the protec-torate was established. He escaped to France via Poland and joined the French Air Force in October 1939 but had not joined an operational unit at the time of the French surrender. He fled again, but to the UK this time, and retrained once again. He did not participate in the Battle of Britain as he joined No. 601 Squadron early in November 1940. He was posted to 313 in June 1941.

Note on the aircraft: TOC 07.09.41. First issued to 129 Sqn on 14.10.41, then to 313 on 25.02.42.

10.04.42   Sgt Vaclav **TRUHLAR**   RAF No.787486   (CZ)/RAF   **AA865**   RY-D   VB   **PoW**

Led by F/L Fajtl, twelve Spitfires took off at 16.50 for an offensive sweep over France as part of an operation involving all of the Hornchurch Wing. Rendezvous was made at West Malling with two other Wings, Kenley and Biggin Hill. The French coast was cros sed at Hardelet. About fifteen miles south of Gravelines, the squadron was attacked out of sun by approximately nine enemy aircraft. In the ensuing combat F/Sgt Foglar claimed a Bf109 as destroyed and F/L Fajtl damaged one while F/L Hájek damaged an Fw190. However, two Spitfires, flown by Sgts Truhlar and Pokorný, did not come back while the rest of the formation landed at base by 18.15. Truhlar was shot down by Fw Karl Willius of 3./JG 26 and was taken prisoner suffering from severe wounds that eventually resulted in his repatriation to the UK in October 1943. When the Germans invaded Czechoslovakia, Truhlar was still under training in the Czechoslovak Air Force and he decided to flee. In November 1939 he enlisted in the French Air Force but once again his training was not complete at the time of the Armistice. He escaped again to the UK with his brother, Jan, who later served with another Czech unit, No. 312 Squadron. Václav, upon the completion of his training, was posted to No. 56 Squadron in April 1941 before joining 313 in June. He recovered from his wounds and served with the post-war Czechoslovakian Air Force but was killed in a flying accident on 10 October 1947 while flying Spitfire SL635.

Note on the aircraft: TOC 17.10.41 and issued to 313 on 26.10.41.

| 10.04.42 | Sgt Frantisek **POKORNÝ** | RAF No.788141 | (CZ)/RAF | **BL480** | | VB | † |

See above. Pokorný was a pre-war Czechoslovak Air Force pilot serving with Air Regiment 4. He was also a member of an aerobatic team led by Nadporučík (Lieutenant) František Novak. Pokorný fled his country, when the Germans invaded, and enlisted in the Polish Air Force. He was captured by the Soviets on 23 September 1939 but released the following year and sailed directly to the UK to join the RAF. He was posted to 313 on completion of his training in February 1942.

Note on the aircraft: TOC 03.01.42. Issued to 313 Sqn 15.01.42.

| 12.04.42 | Sgt Otakar **KRESTA** | RAF No.787457 | (CZ)/RAF | **AD384** | RY-P | VB | **PoW** |

With No. 64 Squadron, 313, led by S/L Mrazek, took off at 12.40 to escort bombers, targeting marshalling yards in Hazebrouck, with the Debden and North Weald Wings (Circus 122). The formation was intercepted by six enemy aircraft about ten miles west of Saint-Omer. Kresta was posted missing from this operation and was shot down by Oberleutnant Rolf Hermichen of 7./JG 26. The Czechs claimed one confirmed victory (F/L Fajtl and Sgt Brázda sharing it) and one damaged by S/L Mrazek. Kresta was later reported as a PoW and spent the rest of the war in various camps - Stalag Luft III in Sagan, Stalag Luft I in Barth, Stalag Luft IVB in Mühlberg and Stalag Luft 355 in Fallingbostel. A pre-war Czechoslovak Air Force pilot, Otakar Kresta escaped to France via Poland after the Germans had taken control of the country. On 2 October 1939 he joined the Armée de l´Air and subsequently served at the bases in Tours and Marrakesh (Morocco). After the Armistice he fled to the United Kingdom to enlist in the RAF. He joined the squadron directly in December 1941 once his training was completed.

Note on the aircraft: TOC 12.10.41. Issued to 313 Sqn 21.10.41.

| 05.05.42 | P/O Vaclav **JÍCHA** | RAF No.66486 | (CZ)/RAF | **BM306** | RY-E | VB | - |

Taking off at 14.40, twelve Spitfires joined the rest of the Hornchurch Wing led by W/C R.P.R. Powell. The squadron flew the high cover for six Bostons targeting Lille (France). They were tasked with flying at 22,000 feet, led by F/L Fejfar, while No. 64 Squadron was flying at 20,000 feet and No. 122 at 21,000 feet. The Hornchurch Wing was later joined by the Debden and North Weald Wings. The formation was attacked by German fighters five miles south-southeast of Furnes. Red 1 (F/L Fejfar) ordered the formation to break and furious dogfights ensued. Fejfar destroyed one Fw190 and claimed another one as a probable. Václav Jícha (Yellow 1) was attacked by four Fw190s and received numerous hits but was able to return to base. The aircraft was later changed from a Cat.B to Cat.E. When Václav Jícha joined the Czechoslovak Air Force, in October 1935, he was already a civilian flying instructor at Liberec. He first served a mechanic before being selected for a pilot course. By 1938 he was serving with Air Regiment 1 as a fighter pilot and was a member of an aerobatic team. When the Germans came to Prague in March 1939 he chose to leave the country and found asylum in France two months later. In June he enlisted in the French Foreign Legion. When France entered the war they opened the doors of their flying schools to former Czech pilots and in December 1939 he was posted to GC I/6 as an NCO. He fought during the Battle of France during which he claimed four confirmed victories (one being shared) and, when he arrived in the UK in July 1940, was among the most experienced Czech pilots the RAF could count on. He was first posted to No. 310 (Czech) Squadron in August but a few days later was obliged to pass through a retraining course at No. 6 OTU to learn RAF procedures. In September 1940 he joined No. 1 Squadron at Wittering where he claimed two shared confirmed victories. He was later posted to No. 17 Squadron in November and was commissioned in April 1941. Shortly after that he joined 313. He left the squadron at the end of his tour in August 1942 and was awarded a well-deserved DFC the following month. In January he became a test pilot with Vickers Armstrong Ltd at Castle Bromwich. Sadly, Jícha did not survive the war. On 1 February 1945 he was flying to Kinloss, Scotland, as a passenger in an Anson (NK945) when the aircraft, piloted by F/L Ferguson, was flown into a snowstorm. The wreckage was not found until the 7th and it is believed that he probably survived the crash but froze to death.

Note on the aircraft: TOC 28.03.42. Issued 313 Sqn 28.03.42.

| | Sgt Karel **PAVLIK** | RAF No.787431 | (CZ)/RAF | **BM261** | | VB | † |

See above. His aircraft crashed near the village of Dranouter. Karel escaped to France via Poland in 1939 and never served with the Czechoslovakian armed forces. In October 1939 he joined the Armée de l´Air and was posted to the base at Istres to under take flying training. When France was defeated he was evacuated to the United Kingdom where he completed his training as a

fighter pilot and was eventually posted to No. 313 Squadron in September 1941. (see also aircraft lost by accident 16.04.42)
<u>Note on the aircraft</u>: TOC 14.03.42. Issued 313 Sqn 14.04.42.

P/O Otmar **Kučera**	RAF No.112548	(cz)/RAF	**BM209**	RY-G	VB		-

See above. Sgt Kučera (Yellow 2) was also attacked by six Fw190s and his aircraft badly hit but he was able to make the journey home. The engine cut from lack of fuel shortly after he crossed the English coast and he made a forced landing at Newchurch on Romney Marsh at 16.40 and escaped slightly injured. Kučera was a former Czechoslovakian Air Force officer serving since 1933. When the Germans occupied the country he was flying with Air Regiment 2. He fled to France via Hungary, Yugoslavia and Lebanon and eventually enlisted in the French Air Force in March 1940. He did not see any action with the French and escaped to England in July. After a refresher course he was posted to No. 111 Squadron in October 1940 as an NCO where he claimed two shared victories before being posted to No. 312 (Czech) Squadron in April 1941. One year later he joined 313 with a commission having also added three confirmed victories and one probable while serving with 312. He stayed with 313 for only a short time and left in June with one more confirmed victory added to his tally (claimed in May). He then served at the training department of the Czechoslovak Air Ministry in London and returned for another tour with 313 on 1 January 1943. He ended his tour as a flight commander with one more enemy aircraft claimed as destroyed. Six months later he returned once again to the squadron to become its last commanding officer before the war's end. He returned in Czechoslovakia in August 1945 after six long years away. He remained with the new Czechoslovakian Air Force after the war and became the CO of Air Fighter Regiment 7 but was arrested by the Communists in January 1949 and spent the following six months in jail. He was eventually released, as no charges could be laid against him, but was demoted to the rank of private. He then worked for many years as a labourer. He was fully rehabilitated following the 'Velvet Revolution' of 1989.
<u>Note on the aircraft</u>: TOC 13.03.42. Issued 313 Sqn 17.04.42.

17.05.42 F/L Stanislav **Fejfar**	RAF No.82545	(cz)/RAF	**BL973**	RY-S	VB		†

Led by the CO, twelve Spitfires took off at 10.40 with the Hornchurch Wing to rendezvous with the North Weald Wing, at 500 feet over Beachy Head, to escort twelve Bostons to Boulogne (Ramrod 33). The formation climbed steadily to 22,000 feet and the French coast was crossed over Hardelet. The target was bombed and the formation set course for Saint-Omer, then to Ambleteuse, the squadron turning slightly to starboard just before arriving there. F/L Fejfar (Blue 1) and Sgt Borkovec (Blue 2) turned to port and lost height. Blue 3 and Blue 4 (P/O Kučera and Sgt Horák) followed and the former called Blue 1 to inform him that the squadron had turned to starboard. No reply was received and sight was lost of Blue 1 and Blue 2 while Blue 3 and 4 regained formation. The two pilots were posted missing once the other aircraft landed at 12.10. Stanislav Fejfar had joined the pre-war Czechoslovakian Air Force in 1932 and, by the time of the invasion of the country in March 1939, was serving with Air Regiment 3. Three months later he fled his country and enlisted in the French Foreign Legion before switching to the Armée de l'Air in October. Re-trained, he was posted to the GC I/6 flying Moranes and in the next few months he would claim two confirmed victories and one probable and retreat to North Africa from where he could escape to Gibraltar. Reaching England, he joined the RAF and was posted at once to the newly-formed No. 310 (Czech) Squadron. He participated in the Battle of Britain and claimed three confirmed victories, one being shared. Due to a health problem he left 310 in October but returned to an operational unit in July 1941 when he joined 313 and served with it until this fateful day. He was shot down by the Gruppenkommandeur III./JG26, Josef Priller. The official tally for Fejfar was seven confirmed victories (two being shared), one probable and three damaged.
<u>Note on the aircraft</u>: TOC 28.02.42. Issued 313 Sqn 30.03.42.

Sgt Miroslav **Borkovec**	RAF No.787528	(cz)/RAF	**BM260**	RY-U	VB		†

See above, shot down by Leutnant Johann Aistleitner of JG 26. Miroslav Borkovec left Czechoslovakia in 1939 to reach France and enlisted, on 9 May 1940, in the Armée de l'Air. After the Armistice he was evacuated to the United Kingdom without having had the opportunity to fight against the Germans. He joined 313 in mid-September 1941 but had to leave it five days later before returning in January 1942.
<u>Note on the aircraft</u>: TOC 29.03.42. Issued 313 Sqn 11.04.42.

02.06.42 Sgt Evzen **Halamazek**	RAF No.787669	(cz)/RAF	**AR397**	RY-D	VB		-

Twelve Spitfires were airborne at 16.40 for Circus 182, with the other squadrons of the Hornchurch Wing, led by the CO, S/L Mrazek. The Hornchurch Wing missed the rendezvous with the two other Wings (Debden and North Weald) so the squadron set course to the target and climbed at the same time. Eventually the two other Wings were joined at 15,000 feet. The Hornchurch Wing followed the other Wings in a right turn near Boulogne and flew mid-channel between Cap Gris Nez and Dover and climbing to 25,000 feet where they flew as a separate formation in visual contact with the other Wings. At that point, 313 was attacked when, at 26,000 feet mid-way between Calais and Boulogne, 12-15 Bf109Fs and Fw190s dived from 30-35,000 feet but quickly disappeared without pressing home an attack. It is believed that Halamazek was hit during this time. A pre-war

Czechoslovak Air Force pilot, Halamazek escaped to France via Poland in 1939 and on 2 October he enlisted in the Armée de l´Air and served with various base defence flights. He was evacuated to the UK in June 1940 and, upon completing his training in November 1940, he joined No. 32 Squadron. In May 1942 he was posted to 313. It is believed that he was shot down by the Fw190s of I./JG 2.

Note on the aircraft: TOC 06.04.42. Issued to 313 Sqn 26.04.42.

15.07.42 Sgt Jan Jeřábek RAF No.787676 (cz)/RAF **AD372** VB †

At 1915, Sgt Jeřábek scrambled as No.2 to F/L Raba to intercept a Ju88. While intercepting the Ju88, his aircraft was hit by return fire and was seen diving and crashing into the sea by F/L Raba. Jeřábek was a pre-war Czechoslovak Air Force pilot. After March 1939 he escaped to France via Poland to enlist in the Armée de l´Air in October 1939 before he was evacuated to the UK. He enlisted in the RAF and became a flight instructor after the end of his training and was awarded an AFM for his service. He began a first operational tour with No. 501 Squadron in April 1942 where he destroyed an Fw190. He arrived at 313 in mid-June.

Note on the aircraft: TOC not recorded. First issued to 317 (Polish) Sqn between 20.10.41 and 01.12.41. Accident, repaired and issued to 313 Sqn 24.06.42.

31.07.42 F/L Miroslav Muzika RAF No.82562 (cz)/RAF **BM452** RY-U VB -

Muzika led six Spitfires of the squadron and left Bolt Head at 10.10 on an ASR mission. During the flight his aircraft developed engine trouble and he was forced to ditch. He was seen in his dinghy and the five remaining aircraft patrolled over him until he was picked up by rescue launch. Jaroslav Muzika initially served as a cavalryman before joining the air force and was serving with Air Regiment 3 at the time of the German invasion. He fled his country in February 1940 and reached France, via Slovakia, Hungary, Yugoslavia and the Middle East. He enlisted in the French Air Force on 12 May 1940 but saw no action before France fell. He escaped to the UK, being re-trained and posted to No. 501 Squadron in April 1941 but joined 313 the following month. He completed his first tour of operations in March 1942 and began a second one with the squadron in July the same year. This tour lasted until August 1943. He did not fly again on operations before the end of the war. He served with the new Czechoslovakian Air Force after the war but he escaped, on 22 January 1949, after the Communist coup, to the United Kingdom on board an Aero C-3 (Siebel Si 204D). He enlisted once again in the RAF and served as a flying instructor until 1958.

Note on the aircraft: TOC 10.04.42. First issued to 154 Sqn on 31.05.42, but passed on to 313 Sqn on 08.06.42.

18.11.42 F/Sgt Jaroslav Hloušek RAF No.787338 (cz)/RAF **AR606** VC †

The squadron took off for a Rhubarb sortie at 15.35, led by S/L Himr, heading for the main Paris-Brest rail line. To the south of Sept Îles, the sections separated. Hloušek was flying as No.2 to P/O Prihoda - Blue section. The formation proceeded to the rail ways between Plouaret and Morlaix and met concentrated flak one mile west of Lannion aerodrome. Blue 1 attacked a gun post without observing results. As he broke away he heard Blue 2 on the RT saying that he was wounded so the section turned north for home. With white smoke coming from Blue 2's engine, Hloušek reported that the temperature was shooting up so Prihoda 1 told him to climb and bail out. He climbed at once to 2,000 feet and was ready to bail out when a stream of black smoke was seen and the aircraft turned and dived straight into the sea 100 yards south of the lighthouse at Les Triagoz. Prihoda circled the spot but could not see anything so returned to England at sea level and arrived back at base at 17.10. Jaroslav Hloušek had joined the squadron in September 1941. He was a pre-war Czechoslovakian airmen still under training when the country was occupied by the Germans and seems to have reached the United Kingdom in 1940.

Note on the aircraft: TOC 20.08.42. Issued to 501 Sqn on 13.09.42, then to 504 Sqn 19.10.42 and to 313 Sqn two days later.

15.01.43 F/O Bedrich Kratkoruky RAF No.110669 (cz)/RAF **AR546** VC †

At 11.15 the twelve Spitfires of the squadron took off led by S/L Himr as part of the Wing (310 & 312 Squadrons) for a Circus operation (No.13). The Wing was serving as cover for Bostons detailed to attack the Cherbourg docks. The Wing climbed across the Channel with No. 310 Squadron flying at the bottom at 22,000 feet, 313 flying in the middle at 23,000 and No. 312 Squadron at 24,000 feet. While crossing the Channel a message was received that the bombers would be three minutes late so, ten miles North of Cap de la Hague, the Wing turned right and swept to the West of Alderney before turning east across the peninsular and crossing the French coast at Cap de Flamanviille to come out over St Vaast. The formation then set course for home. During the operation, two pilots collided in the air while making a turn into the sun. Kratkoruky was able to keep some control and was followed down towards the coast by W/O F. Vasicek and was seen to make a good landing on the sea about fifteen miles south of Portland. The aircraft soon sank but neither the pilot or dinghy were seen. The ASR launched was not successful and his body was never found. Bedrich Kratkoruky was a former Czechoslovakian Air Force pilot who was serving with Air Regiment 4 when the Germans occupied his country. He fled Czechoslovakia and soon reached France where he enlisted first in the French Foreign Legion and then in the Armée de l'Air soon after France entered the war. He fought as an NCO with

GC.III/3 on Moranes and Dewoitines and scored several times to end the campaign with three shared confirmed victories and one probable. He escaped to England and was posted to No. 1 Squadron once his training was completed. There he claimed two more victories during the spring of 1941 and left the unit in January 1942 when his tour ended. He had joined 313 in August 1942, now as an officer, for his second tour.

`Note on the aircraft: TOC 17.07.42. Issued 313 Sqn 26.07.42.`

| | F/Sgt Josef **BLÁHA** | RAF No.788010 | (cz)/RAF | **EP449** | VB | † |

See above. Last seen spinning down into the sea and no subsequent trace was seen of him or his aircraft. Before the war Josef Bláha served with the Czechoslovakian Air Force. In 1939 he escaped to Poland where he joined the Polish Air Force. He was captured by the Red Army on 23 September but was later released and reached the United Kingdom in 1941. He was posted to 313 in July 1942.

`Note on the aircraft: TOC 26.06.42. Issued 313 Sqn 24.07.42.`

| **27.02.43** | F/L Miroslav **STUSAK** | RAF No.82530 | (cz)/RAF | **AR520** | VC | † |

S/L Himr took off at 13.50 leading two sections with Studak leading the second section. The operation was a close escort to Fortresses bombing Brest. Intercepted by Fw190s, Studak was shot down by Uffz. Heinz Butteweg of 8./JG 2 and killed fifteen mile north of Île of Batz. His body was never recovered. His engine was hit and, as the temperature began to rise, he decided to bail out. His parachute opened normally but no sign of life was seen after he hit the water. A pre-war Czechoslovakian Air Force pilot, he escaped from his country when it was occupied by Germany. He reached France via the Middle East. He enlisted in the Armée de l'Air in February 1940 but was evacuated to England in June 1940 without having seen action. He had been serving the squadron since August 1942.

`Note on the aircraft: TOC 07.07.42. Issued 313 Sqn 30.07.42.`

| **06.03.43** | F/O Josef **PRIHODA** | RAF No.110307 | (cz)/RAF | **BP862** | VC | † |

No. 313 Squadron was taking part in an escort of fifteen American Liberators tasked with bombing Brest (Ramrod 56). The escort also comprised Nos. 130 and 602 Squadrons. Twelve Spitfires were detailed, led by S/L Himr, and took off at 13.25. While en route, the British fighters were suddenly intercepted by Fw190s which shot down one Spitfire of 130 Squadron. The squadron left the formation to engage the enemy and, during the ensuing combat, while the other squadrons reformed to escort the bombers home, F/Sgt Slepica claimed one Fw190 as damaged before 313 returned to the escort formation. P/O Prihoda was posted missing from this sortie and nothing was known about him when the squadron returned to base at 15.20. It was later found that he had been shot down by Fw Friedrich May of III./JG 2. Josef Prihoda was a pre-war Czechoslovakian Air Force pilot. After the occupation of Czechoslovakia he escaped to France via Poland. He first served with the French Foreign Legion and when the war broke out he was allowed to enlist in the Armée de l´Air. In November he joined ERC 571, a flight which became 6éme Escadrille of GC.III/4. After the Armistice he was evacuated to the United Kingdom via Casablanca and Gibraltar. After being re-trained he was posted to No. 1 Squadron in October 1940. With this unit he claimed one confirmed, two probables and one damaged aircraft before, in September 1941, he was posted to No. 111 Squadron, commissioned and increased his tally by another confirmed victory and one more probable. In April 1942 he was posted to 313 and left in July at the completion of his tour. In September he was called back for another tour, joined 313 again and was awarded the DFC the following month.

`Note on the aircraft: TOC 24.02.42. 66 Sqn 16.04.42 then accident 22.05.42. Repaired and issued to 313 Sqn date non recorded.`

| **08.03.43** | F/L Benignus **STEFAN** | RAF No.87624 | (cz)/RAF | **AR547** | VC | † |

The Czech Wing made a rendezvous over Exeter with the squadron providing eleven Spitfires for this bomber escort operation, Ramrod 57, led by the CO. They took off at 13.10. While ten miles east of Paimpol, F/L Stefan was surprised by an Fw190 flown by Uffz Heinz Butteweg of 8./JG 2 and was last seen going down in a shallow dive, weaving, but under control. A pre-war Czechoslovakian Air Force pilot, he escaped to Poland in August 1939 and enlisted in the Polish Air Force three days before the beginning of the war. Captured by the Soviets on 23 September 1939, he was released in August 1940 and reached England in October. He was posted to No. 310 (Czech) Squadron in June 1942 but was posted to 313 one week later.

`Note on the aircraft: TOC 17.07.42. Issued 313 Sqn 30.07.42.`

| **24.09.43** | P/O John B. **COCHRANE** | RAF No.142065 | RAF | **W3895** | RY-O | VB | † |

Led by W/C Doležal, who was flying with the squadron, eleven Spitfires took off at 12.45 to escort twelve Mitchells which were planning to bomb a target located south of Brest. Bf110s tried to intercept and 313 was able to shoot down one Bf110 (confirmed) with another being declared as a probable. However P/O Cochrane did not return and was presumed to have been shot down. It is thought that he was able to bale out. Cochrane was among the few British pilots to be posted to the squadron in July

1943 to reinforce the unit due to the shortage of Czech pilots.

Note on the aircraft: TOC 17.09.41. Issued 92 Sqn 22.09.41, then 417 (RCAF) Sqn 07.02.42, 242 (Canadian) Sqn 28.03.42 until 03.02.43, 504 Sqn 02.09.43 and 313 Sqn 22.09.43.

	S/L Jaroslav **HIMR**	RAF No.81891	(CZ)/RAF	**BP856**	RY-H	VC	-

See above. Jaroslav Himr was serving with the squadron in June 1942 on his second tour of operations. He was a pre-war Czechoslovakian pilot serving with Air Regiment 3. In February 1940 he fled to France via Slovakia, Hungary and Yugoslavia but arrived too late to take part in the fighting that spring even though he enlisted in the Armée de l'Air on 26 March. He was evacuated to England and was posted to the newly-formed No. 310 (Czech) Squadron in July pending his training on Hurricanes and did not fly operationally. Sent to No. 6 OTU to be re-trained, he joined No. 79 Squadron in September 1940 but left the following month for No. 56 Squadron where he remained until June 1941. That month he was posted to No. 601 Squadron and ended his first tour with this unit in December as a flight commander.

Note on the aircraft: TOC 10.02.42. First with 66 Sqn between 17.04.42 and 24.07.42, damaged and repaired. To 312 (Czech) Sqn 31.05.43, 504 05.07.43 and 313 Sqn 22.09.43.

27.09.43	Sgt Tomas **ZRNIK**	RAF No.787374	(CZ)/RAF	**AR547**		VC	†

Eleven Spitfires took off at 09.45 for a close escort to 72 Marauders heading to Beauvais aerodrome in France (Ramrod 250). They were intercepted by enemy aircraft (JG26). In the ensuing combat, three Fw190s were claimed as damaged (Sgt Hlučka, F/L Hochmal, F/O Masaryk) but Tomáš Zrník was absent when the Czechs returned to base at 11.55. Zrník was a former pre-war Czechoslovakian Air Force ground crew who escaped to France in 1939. He joined the French Air Force in March 1940 but did not receive a posting while in French uniform. He was evacuated to the UK, enlisted in the RAF and served as ground crew with No. 312 (Czech) Squadron for a while. Later selected for a fighter pilot course, he joined the squadron in January 1943 on completion of his training.

Note on the aircraft: TOC 17.07.42. Issued 313 Sqn 30.07.42.

19.04.44	W/O Arnost **MRTVY**	RAF No.787187	(CZ)/RAF	**MJ558**		LF.IXC	-

In the afternoon, the squadron left for Manston. At 18.00 it took off under F/L Hochmal's command to escort 72 B-26 Marauders targeting the railways at Malines (Ramrod 753). Before reaching the target about twenty Bf109s were encountered but no side had any success. While passing over the target the squadron was again attacked, but this time by Fw190s, and W/O Mrtvý was presumed to have been shot down by Oblt Wolfgang Neu, Staffelkapitän of 4./JG 26. The rest of the formation returned to base at 20.00. A pre-war Czechoslovakian pilot Arnošt Mrtvý escaped to France via Poland during summer 1939. He joined the Armée de l'Air in October and served in the south-west of France and was eventually evacuated to England in June 1940. He enlisted in the RAF, was re-trained and posted to No. 24 Squadron for a short time before, in April 1941, he joined No. 257 Squadron. In July he was posted to No. 65 Squadron then to 313 the following month where he served until the end of his tour in August 1943. In February 1944 he returned to the squadron for another tour. (see also accidental losses 11.03.44)

Note on the aircraft: TOC 12.12.43. Issued 313 Sqn 24.01.44.

20.04.44	W/O Alexander **WEMYSS**	RAF No.1344405	RAF	**MK122**	RY-A	LF.IXC	**PoW**

Led by F/L A. Hochmal, twelve Spitfires took off at 19.10 for Ramrod 761 in order to escort bombers over the Abbeville area. While the squadron was turning over France, W/O Wemyss broke formation and was not seen again and was later on reported in a PoW camp. No further incident was reported and the squadron landed at 20.50. Alexander Wemyss had been serving with the squadron since July 1943 and was among the few RAF pilots to be posted in during the summer of 1943 to keep the squadron operational.

Note on the aircraft: TOC 10.01.44. Issued 313 Sqn 22.01.44.

25.10.44	F/Sgt William H. **HALLATT**	RAF No.1339064	RAF	**ML207**		HF.IXC	-

For Ramrod 1347, twelve Spitfires led by S/L Kasal took off at 14.00 (with a stop at Bradwell to refuel) to provide escort to 600 Halifaxes and Lancasters targeting Essen in Germany. All aircraft returned safely at 17.00 except William Hallatt who bailed out near Bruges, Belgium, after reporting a shortage of fuel. Hallatt had been serving with the squadron since May and left in December 1944. His subsequent postings are unknown.

Note on the aircraft: TOC 13.04.44. Issued 74 Sqn 04.05.44, then 312 (Czech) Sqn 28.09.44 and 313 Sqn 05.10.44.

29.11.44	Sgt Bruce **MCPHEE**	CAN./R.171408	RCAF	**ML353**		HF.IXC	-

For Ramrod 1382, twelve aircraft led by F/L R. Wood took off at 13.15 to provide escort, on penetration and withdrawal, to 270

Lancasters bombing targets at Dortmund. On return ML353, short of fuel, crash landed at Cappes near Calais. The pilot was unhurt. Bruce McPhee, a Canadian from Quebec, was one of the four Canadians posted to the squadron in June 1944. Posted to No. 412 Squadron early in December, he was eventually commissioned as J92600. He was forced down in enemy territory on 20 January 1945 (Spitfire PV352), after having been hit by flak during an armed recce, and became a PoW at Stalag Luft III.
<u>Note on the aircraft</u>: TOC 19.04.44. Issued 313 Sqn 05.10.44.

| **28.01.45** | Sgt Jaroslav **ŘEHOŘ** | RAF No.788319 | (CZ)/RAF | **NH450** | RY-R | HF.IXC | - |

Seven Spitfires led by F/L F. Masarik took off at 12.50 as part of a Wing escort to cover the rear of the bomber stream on with drawal after the 150 Lancasters had bombed the marshalling yards at Cologne (Ramrod 1444). It was not a lucky mission as three aircraft returned early due to technical trouble and for F/Sgt Řehoř the situation became critical when his aircraft ran out of fuel after 2.30 hours of flight. He was obliged to land at B.67 - Ursel (Belgium) at 15.12. Unfortunately he landed with a strong cross wind and lost control and crashed. He was not without luck, however, as he escaped injury. Jaroslav Řehoř was former ground crew who was selected to become a pilot in 1943. He had been serving with the squadron since November 1944.
<u>Note on the aircraft</u>: TOC 28.05.44. Issued 312 (Czech) Sqn 05.09.44, then 313 (Czech) Sqn 05.10.44.

| **01.02.45** | F/L John A.H. **PINNY** | RAF No.129145 | RAF | **NH148** | RY-O | HF.IXC | † |

Led by the CO, twelve aircraft were airborne at 15.10 to take part in RAMROD 1448 and provide cover and escort on withdrawal to the 160 Lancasters bombing a target east of Rheydt. Over the target, Pinny's engine cut and he glided the machine over Allied lines but was killed when he crashed into trees approximately twenty miles south-west of Eindhoven (Netherlands). John Pinny had been serving with the squadron since September 1943. He had previously served with No. 41 Squadron between October 1941 and June 1942 before sailing to Malta where he joined No. 603 Squadron and, in July, No.1435 Flight. During his stay in Malta his tally reached two confirmed victories and one probable. In October he was posted back to the UK after having survived a crash off Gibraltar in Liberator AL516 of No. 511 Squadron (fourteen killed). He was commissioned and was posted to No. 313 Squadron in September 1943 for another tour.
<u>Note on the aircraft</u>: TOC 28.04.44. Issued 312 (Czech) Sqn 30.05.44 then 313 Sqn 05.10.44.

Total : 31

APPENDIX VI
AIRCRAFT LOST IN ACCIDENTS

SPITFIRE

| **27.05.41** | Sgt Josef **GUTVALD** | RAF No.787349 | (CZ)/RAF | **R7163** | | IA | † |

During a training flight, the Spitfire dived into the ground for unknown reasons at Uckerby near Scorton, Yorkshire, killing its pilot. He didn't serve with the pre-war Czechoslovakian Air Force but enlisted in Aviation Group of the Czechoslovak Army in Agde (France). After the fall of France he escaped to the United Kingdom where he joined the RAF and after some training was posted in October 1940 to No. 43 Squadron until 6 May when he joined No. 3 Squadron for a mere twelve days before he joined 313 only to be killed nine days after his arrival.
<u>Note on the aircraft</u>: TOC unrecorded, but first flight 01.03.41. Issued 452 (RAAF) Sqn 24.04.41, then 313 Sqn 20.05.41.

| **26.06.41** | F/O Karel **KASAL** | RAF No.81893 | (CZ)/RAF | **R6709** | RY-R | IA | - |

Operational and practice flying continued all day in good weather. Kasal crash landed his Spitfire at Martlesham Heath, due to a lack of flying discipline, and damaged a Hurricane parked there. He suffered head injuries and contusions and was taken to East Suffolk and Ipswich Hospital. A Czech born in Austria, he served in the pre-war Czechoslovakian Air Force and by 1939 he was flying with Air Regiment 6. He fled to France and joined the French Air France but saw no action. He escaped to Great Britain and enlisted in the RAF. He completed his training and was posted to No. 607 Squadron in November 1940. In May he joined 313 but left for No. 312 (Czech) Squadron in June 1942 and stayed there until November when he was posted out at the end of his tour. His rest was short as he started another tour in January with 312 and flew until June 1944. A third tour followed in September 1944 when he took command of 313 for several months before leaving in November. In June 1945 he returned to 312 as it returned to Czechoslovakia.

Note on the aircraft: TOC 09.06.40. Issued 54 Sqn 12.06.40.. 41 Sqn 22.02.41, then 452 (RAAF) Sqn 09.04.41 and finally 313 Sqn 16.06.41.

22.01.42   Sgt Blazej **KONALVLINA**   RAF No.788039   (CZ)/RAF   **AD547**   VB   †

While practicing combat with his section leader, Sgt Špaček, it is understood that Sgt Konavlina lost control and he was seen to crash into ground near Hornchurch. Konavlina had fled his country and, unlike many other Czechs, he reached the United Kingdom directly where he enlisted in the RAF. He was first posted to No.1 Squadron in July 1941 before joining No. 258 Squadron in August. He stayed there less than two months before being posted to No. 54 Squadron in October and then No. 65 Squadron in November before eventually settling with 313 on 2 January. A court of inquiry was formed to investigate Konavlina's death and Otto Špaček was blamed for a lack of flying discipline during this flight and sentenced. A pre-war Czechoslovakian pilot, he fought with the French flying Bloch 152s with GC.I/8 and claimed two victories, one being shared, but was shot down twice including once by friendly anti-aircraft fire. See 06.03.44 for further details.

Note on the aircraft: TOC 30.10.41. Issued 313 Sqn 06.11.41.

16.04.42   Sgt Karel **PAVLIK**   RAF No.787431   (CZ)/RAF   **BM115**   VB   -

Sgt Pavlík was returning from an air firing practice flight when he stalled at nine feet while coming in to land on the runway. The aircraft struck the ground heavily and the undercarriage collapsed. It was 15.30. Pavlík was killed with the squadron three weeks later. (see operational losses 05.05.42).

Note on the aircraft: TOC 28.02.42. Issued 313 Sqn 14.04.42.

04.06.43   F/O Jaroslav **ČERMÁK**   RAF No.61546   (CZ)/RAF   **AR512**   VC   †

Having taken off with three other pilots at 10.05 for a practice low level attack on a train, Čermák got too close to the target and hit it at high speed with the wing tip of his Spitfire. The aircraft crashed leaving no chance of survival for the pilot. Jaroslav Čermák was a former Intelligence Officer who had served in this position with No. 310 (Czech) Squadron. Later re-trained as a fighter pilot, his first operational posting was to the squadron in April.

Note on the aircraft: TOC 29.06.42. Issued 313 Sqn 26.08.42.

12.09.43   F/Sgt Jack E. **GREEN**   RAF No.1335503   RAF   **AA843**   VB   †

Jack Green took off at 14.40 for a training flight but crashed when returning to base forty minutes later. The aircraft struck high ground while flying level in cloud. Jack Green was one of the British pilots who joined the squadron in July 1943 due to the lack of Czech personnel.

Note on the aircraft: TOC 29.09.41. Issued 313 Sqn 29.07.43, previously served with Nos. 72, 421 (RCAF), 350 (Belgian), 93, 610, 131 & 310 (Czech) Sqns.

06.03.44   F/Sgt Otto **SPACEK**   RAF No.787671   (CZ)/RAF   **MK131**   RY-D   LF.IXC   -

F/Sgt Špaček took off from Mendlesham at 11.00 to make a cine-gun practice flight. The engine cut while taking off. He tried to stop the Spitfire but in applying the brakes the aircraft swung and tipped-up. Otto Špaček was a pre-war Czechoslovakian Air Force pilot and served with Air Regiment 3. In 1939 he fled to France via Poland and enlisted in the French Air Force. He was retrained and joined the fighter unit GC I/8 in March 1940 flying the MB.152. He was shot down once on 11 May but had his revenge on 6 June when he claimed a Bf109 as destroyed and shared a Do17. However, six days later, he was shot down again, but by friendly anti-aircraft fire this time, and injured. He was evacuated to the UK a couple of days later. Retrained once more, he eventually joined the recently formed No. 312 (Czech) Squadron in October 1940 and was then posted to No. 615 Squadron in April 1941. In June he joined 313 and stayed until June 1943 when his tour came to an end. He returned to the squadron in December 1943 for another tour and served with it until the end of war (by which time he had received his commission). He served in the post-war Czechoslovakian Air Force with Air Regiment 12 but had to flee from his country again when the Communists took over. He eventually settled in Canada.

Note on the aircraft: TOC 02.02.44. Issued 313 Sqn 15.02.44.

11.03.44   W/O Arnost **MRTVY**   RAF No.787187   (CZ)/RAF   **MK173**   RY-E   LF.IXC   †

The squadron carried out various training flights on this day. At 9.50 Mrtvý took off with other pilots to carry out an Army co-

operation exercise but fifteen minutes after take-off his Spitfire encountered engine trouble and he made a forced landing near Mildenhall. He escaped injury but was killed one month later on operations (see the respective entry for personal details).
Note on the aircraft: TOC 29.01.44. Issued 313 Sqn 12.02.44.

| 15.03.44 | Sgt Jindrich **KONVICKA** | RAF No.788221 | (CZ)/RAF | **MK609** | RY-X | LF.IXC | - |

At 15.00 Sgt Konvička took off for bombing practice. Ten minutes later Konvička had to return to base due to ASI failure. With no accurate way to confirm his airspeed, he made his landing approach at too high a speed and overshot the landing before hitting a dispersal pen. Konvička had joined the squadron the previous month on completion of his training. In May he was posted to No. 312 (Czech) Squadron where he served until the end of his tour in December 1944.
Note on the aircraft: TOC No.8 MU 26.03.44, issued No.441 Sqn 28.09.44. Served also with No.56 Sqn.

| 26.04.44 | F/L Jan **LASKA** | RAF No.82558 | (CZ)/RAF | **MJ979** | RY-O | LF.IXC | † |
| | F/Sgt Frantisek **FANTA** | RAF No.788113 | (CZ)/RAF | **MK344** | RY-V | LF.IXC | † |

The squadron made only one sortie that day, a practice bombing with live bombs dropped in the sea off Selsey Bill. During this exercise, while the aircraft were reforming after bombing, F/Sgt Fanta collided with F/L Laska and both aircraft crashed. Laska was found alive but died shortly afterwards while Fanta was found dead. Jan Laska was a pre-war Czechoslovakian pilot who joined the RAF during the summer of 1940 and first served with No. 312 (Czech) Squadron between October 1940 and July 1941. He then joined No. 245 Squadron for a short time before he transferred to No. 32 Squadron where he remained until the following July when he was posted to 313. He completed his first tour in April 1943 and returned to the squadron for another tour in October. František Fanta was only trained in the UK and had joined the squadron in October on completion of his training.
Note on the aircraft:
MJ979: TOC 07.01.44. Issued 313 Sqn 22.01.44.
MK344: TOC 04.02.44. Issued 313 Sqn 16.02.44.

| 15.07.44 | F/O Robert E. **DODDS** | RAF No.172864 | RAF | **MB763** | DU-Z | VII | - |

That day, Robert Dodds took off from Skeabrae for a type experience flight. After twenty minutes, he returned to base but misjudged his speed and overshot the runway on landing and tipped the Spitfire up on its nose. Robert Dodds, who escaped injury in the accident, had joined the squadron in August 1943 from No. 616 Squadron. He left the squadron in February 1945 at the end of his tour.
Note on the aircraft: TOC 20.07.43. Officially on charge to SF Skaebrae. Previously with 312 (Czech), 118 & 453 (RAAF) Sqns.

TIGER MOTH

| 19.01.45 | - | | - | - | **AX783** | - | - |

While stationed at Bradwell Bay, at 07.35 it was blown by a gale, gusting to 70 mph, to the rear of the hangar causing considerable damage.
Note on the aircraft: Formely G-AFMC impressed in July 1940. Issued 313 Sqn 03.10.44, previously with RAF Topcliffe, 434 (RCAF) and 312 (Czeh) Sqns.

Total : 13
including 12 combat aircraft

APPENDIX VII
Aircraft serial numbers matching with individual letters

RY-A
R6623 (*Spitfire I*)
MK122 (*Spitfire IX*)
RY-B
NH458 (*Spitfire IX*)
RY-C
ML171 (*Spitfire IX*)
RY-D
P7502 (*Spitfire II*)
AA865, AR397, BM357 (*Spitfire V*)
MK131, MK842 (*Spitfire IX*)
RY-E
AD390, BL769, BM306 (*Spitfire V*)
MK694 (*Spitfire IX*)
RY-F
R6604 (*Spitfire II*)
P7834 (*Spitfire II*)
AB916, BM117, BM127 (*Spitfire V*)
RY-G
BM209, EP129, EP575 (*Spitfire V*)
MJ963 (*Spitfire IX*)
RY-H
P7601, P7973 (*Spitfire II*)
AD391, BP856 (*Spitfire V*)

RY-I
ML184 (*Spitfire IX*)
RY-J
EP664 (*Spitfire V*)
MK205, NH459 (*Spitfire IX*)
RY-K
AB276, AD192, AR432, EP394 (*Spitfire V*)
RY-L
AD361 (*Spitfire V*)
RY-M
P8076 (*Spitfire II*)
AB142 (*Spitfire V*)
RY-N
NH250 (*Spitfire IX*)
RY-O
W3895, AA833 (*Spitfire V*)
MJ979, NH148 (*Spitfire IX*)
RY-P
AD384 (*Spitfire V*)
RY-Q
EP660 (*Spitfire V*)
RY-R
R6702 (*Spitfire I*)
MK320, NH450 (*Spitfire IX*)

RY-S
P8174 (*Spitfire II*)
AD424, BL973, EP644 (*Spitfire V*)
RY-T
P8259 (*Spitfire II*)
BL581 (*Spitfire V*)
RY-U
BM260, BM452 (*Spitfire V*)
ML259 (*Spitfire IX*)
RY-V
R7205 (*Spitfire I*)
MK344 (*Spitfire IX*)
RY-W
P8657 (*Spitfire II*)
AA757 (*Spitfire V*)
RY-X
W3962, AR436 (*Spitfire V*)
MK609 (*Spitfire IX*)
RY-Y
EP661 (*Spitfire V*)
RY-Z
P8537, AB249, AD380 (*Spitfire V*)

APPENDIX VIII
List of known pilots posted or attached to the Squadron

RAF
N. Aspinal, RAF No.1337643
J. Bedna, RAF No.787716, *Czech*
V. Bergman, RAF No.81884, *Czech*
F. Bernard, RAF No.120209, *Czech*
J. Blaha, RAF No.788010, *Czech*
F. Bönisch, RAF No.788038, *Czech*
M. Borkovec, RAF No.787528, *Czech*
P. Brazda, RAF No.787673, *Czech*
R. Brhel, RAF No.788424, *Czech*
R.A.A. Cannon, RAF No.142064
A.V. Chandler, RAF No.1319672
J.B. Cochrane, RAF No.142065
A.R. Costello, RAF No.41781
K. Cap, RAF No.787544, *Czech*
J. Cermak, RAF No.84666, *Czech*
J. Cermak, RAF No.61546, *Czech*
J. Cermak, RAF No.787363, *Czech*
LJ. Dalziel, RAF No.186903
I.F.R. Dickinson, RAF No. 169065
J. Dobrovolny, RAF No.146768, *Czech*
J. Dohnal, RAF No.787690

R.E. Doods, RAF No.172864
K. Drbohlav, RAF No. 81906, *Czech*
B. Dubec, RAF No.787684, *Czech*
F. Epstein, RAF No.788668, Czech
F. Fajtl, RAF No.82544, *Czech*
F. Fanta, RAF No.788113, *Czech*
S. Fejfar, RAF No.82545, *Czech*
V. Foglar, RAF No.130857, *Czech*
T.W. Gillen, RAF No.70245
A.R. Glen, RAF No.184693
J.E. Green, RAF No.1335503
J. Gutvald, RAF No.787349, *Czech*
V. Hajek, RAF No.87617, *Czech*
E. Halamasek, RAF No.787669, *Czech*
W.H. Hallatt, RAF No.1339064
M. Havlicek, RAF No.788161, *Czech*
J. Himr, RAF No.81891, *Czech*
J. Hlouzek, RAF No.787338, *Czech*
S. Hlucka, RAF No.787058, *Czech*
K. Hoch, RAF No.788455, *Czech*
A. Hochmal, RAF No.82548, Czech
V. Horak, RAF No.787561, *Czech*

O. Hruby, RAF No.117341, *Czech*
E.R. Jacobs, RAF No.186123
J. Jaske, RAF No.83226, *Czech*
E. Jelinek, RAF No.654731, *Czech*
J. Jerabek, RAF No.787676, *Czech*
V. Jicha, RAF No.66486, *Czech*
J. Jilek, RAF No.787467, *Czech*
K. Kasal, RAF No.81893, *Czech*
J. Kauer, RAF No.787634, *Czech*
J.I. Kilmartin, RAF No.39793
B. Kimlicka, RAF No.82553, *Czech*
P. Kocfelda, RAF No.787471, *Czech*
J. Kohout, RAF No.787389, *Czech*
B. Konvalina, RAF No.788039, *Czech*
J. Konvicka, RAF No.788221, *Czech*
J. Konvicka, RAF No.788221, *Czech*
F. Kotiba, RAF No.787385, *Czech*
B. Kratkoruky, RAF No.110669, *Czech*
O. Kresta, RAF No.787457, *Czech*
F. Kruta, RAF No.787674, *Czech*
J. Kucera, RAF No.103533, *Czech*
O. Kucera, RAF No.112548, *Czech*

J. **Kukucka**, RAF No.654729, *Czech*
O. **Kylar,** RAF No.788485, *Czech*
J. **Laska**, RAF No.82558, *Czech*
G.E.T. **Lawley**, RAF No.1218543
D.P.A. **Leslie**, RAF No.1530478
K.C. **Maslen**, RAF No.184349
F. **Mares**, RAF No.787653, *Czech*
F. **Masarik,** RAF No.120196, *Czech*
J. **Marsik**, RAF No.154422, *Czech*
M. **Mecir**, RAF No.146067, *Czech*
V. **Michalek**, RAF No.68727, *Czech*
J.S. **Mitchell**
F. **Mlejnecky**, RAF No.787503, *Czech*
J. **Motycka**, RAF No.82623, *Czech*
O.C. **Moxon**, RAF No.1377447
B. **Mraz**, RAF No.787603, *Czech*
K. **Mrazek**, RAF No.82561, *Czech*
A. **Mrtvy**, RAF No.787187, *Czech*
J. **Muzika**, RAF No.82562, *Czech*
M. **Nagy**, RAF No.654738, *Czech*
V. **Palicka**, RAF No.787029, *Czech*
K. **Pavlik**, RAF No.787431, *Czech*
K. **Perina**, RAF No.788140, *Czech*
J.A.H. **Pinny**, RAF No.129145
J. **Pipa**, RAF No.145101, *Czech*
F. **Pokorny**, RAF No.788141, *Czech*
V. **Prerost**, RAF No.787504, *Czech*
J. **Prihoda**, RAF No.110307, *Czech*

R. **Ptacek**, RAF No.787434, *Czech*
V. **Raba**, RAF No.82569, *Czech*
S. **Rejthar**, RAF No.82570, *Czech*
A.O. **Reynolds**, RAF No.139519
D.R. **Reynolds**, RAF No.537337
E.S. **Roberts**, RAF No.656038
J. **Ruprecht**, RAF No.788347, *Czech*
V. **Ruprecht**, RAF No.787526, *Czech*
J. **Rehor**, RAF No.788319, *Czech*
J. **Reznicek**, RAF No.159266, *Czech*
G. **Simon**
G.L. **Sinclair**, RAF No.39644
J. **Skopa**, RAF No.788208, *Czech*
K. **Slama**, RAF No.83240, *Czech*
J. **Slepica**, RAF No.788033, *Czech*
F. **Steiner**, RAF No.788107, *Czech*
J. **Stivar**, RAF No.184654, *Czech*
M. **Stoces**, RAF No.787376, *Czech*
C. **Stojan**, RAF No.189480, *Czech*
K. **Stryk**, RAF No.787805, *Czech*
J. **Sika**, RAF No. 787382, *Czech*
V. **Slouf**, RAF No.112547, *Czech*
E. **Smolka**, RAF No.787045, *Czech*
O. **Spacek**, RAF No.177614, *Czech*
B. **Stefan**, RAF No.87624, *Czech*
J. **Stefan**, RAF No.787599, *Czech*
K. **Stefanek**, RAF No.788046, *Czech*
M. **Stusak**, RAF No.82530, *Czech*

P.H. **Tidy**, RAF No.1332605
V. **Truhlar**, RAF No.787486, *Czech*
K. **Valasek**, RAF No.787485, *Czech*
J. **Valenta**, RAF No.787681, *Czech*
F. **Vancl**, RAF No.87628, *Czech*
F. **Vavrinek**, RAF No.174310, *Czech*
B. **Velvarsky**, RAF No.788543, *Czech*
A. **Vendl**, RAF No.787685, *Czech*
O. **Vychodil**, RAF No.182286, *Czech*
K. **Vykoukal**, RAF No.81902, *Czech*
A. **Wemyss**, RAF No.1344405
P. **West**, RAF No.171949
R. **Wood**, RAF No.121525
L. **Zadrobilek**, RAF No.787552, *Czech*
A. **Zalesky**, RAF No.787439, *Czech*
M. **Zauf**, RAF No.787496, *Czech*
K. **Zouhar**, RAF No.130858, *Czech*
T. **Zrnik**, RAF No.787374, *Czech*

RCAF
A.M. **Davidson**, Can./J.12386
A.K. **Keats**, Can./R.100869
S.W. **McCracken**, Can./J.89406
B. **McPhee**, Can./R.171408

USAAF
A.C. **Gaydos**, T221326

APPENDIX IX
ROLL OF HONOUR
✝

AIRCREW

Name	Service No	Rank	Age	Origin	Date	Serial
BLAHA, Josef	RAF No.788010	F/Sgt	28	(CZ)/RAF	15.01.43	EP449
BONISH, Frantisek	RAF No.788038	Sgt	28	(CZ)/RAF	23.02.42	AD391
BORKOVEC, Miroslav	RAF No.787528	Sgt	25	(CZ)/RAF	17.05.42	BM260
CERMAK, Jaroslav	RAF No.61546	F/O	26	(CZ)/RAF	04.06.43	AR512
COCHRANE, John Blair	RAF No.142065	P/O	n/k	RAF	24.09.43	W3895
FANTA, Frantisek	RAF No.788113	F/Sgt	24	(CZ)/RAF	26.04.44	MK344
FEJFAR, Stanislav	RAF No.82545	F/L	29	(CZ)/RAF	17.05.42	BL973
GREEN, Jack Edwin	RAF No.1335503	F/Sgt	21	RAF	12.09.43	AA843
GUTVALD, Josef	RAF No.787349	Sgt	29	(CZ)/RAF	27.05.41	R7163
HLOUSEK, Jaroslav	RAF No.787338	F/Sgt	22	(CZ)/RAF	18.11.42	AR606
JERABEK, Jan	RAF No.787676	Sgt	22	(CZ)/RAF	15.07.42	AD372
KONALVLINA, Blazaj	RAF No.788039	Sgt	23	(CZ)/RAF	22.01.42	AD547
KRATKORUKY, Bedrich	RAF No.110669	F/O	29	(CZ)/RAF	15.01.43	AR546
LASKA, Jan	RAF No.82558	F/L	29	(CZ)/RAF	26.04.44	MJ979
MICHALEK, Vladimir	RAF No.68727	P/O	24	(CZ)/RAF	27.03.42	AD197
MRTVY, Arnost	RAF No.787187	W/O	22	(CZ)/RAF	11.03.44	MK173
PAVLIK, Karel	RAF No.787431	Sgt	23	(CZ)/RAF	05.05.42	BM261
PINNY, John Anthony Hurst	RAF No.129145	F/O	24	RAF	01.02.44	NH148
POKORNY, Frantisek	RAF No.788141	Sgt	25	(CZ)/RAF	10.04.42	BL480
PRIHODA, Josef	RAF No.110307	F/O	29	(CZ)/RAF	06.03.43	BP862
STEFAN, Benignus	RAF No.87624	F/L	25	(CZ)/RAF	08.03.43	AR547
STUSAK, Miroslav	RAF No.82530	F/L	31	(CZ)/RAF	27.02.43	AR520
VALENTA, Josef	RAF No.787681	Sgt	24	(CZ)/RAF	11.01.42	AD424
ZAUF, Miroslav	RAF No.787496	Sgt	27	(CZ)/RAF	18.03.42	AA869
ZRNIK, Tomas	RAF No.787374	Sgt	23	(CZ)/RAF	27.09.43	AR547

Total : 25

Czechoslovakia: 22, United Kigndom : 3

GROUNDCREW
Nil

n/k: not known

Above, Spitfire Mk. I X4163 served with various units during the Battle of Britain before being issued to 313 in June 1941. By mid-41 the Mk. I was obsolete but was perfect for new squadrons to work up to operational standard leaving the Mk. V, the new standard mark, for operations. X4163 went directly to an OTU in October when 313 moved to the Mk. V. Below, another Mk. I, X4653/RY-D, which left the squadron at the end of August 1941.

Training contains some risk, however, and some Mk. Is left the squadron earlier than planned. R7205/RY-V, for example, was damaged on landing on 9 August. It was sent back for repairs where it was converted to a Mk. Va. The serial partially overpainted by the fuselage band is repeated at the top of the band. *(Jiri Rajlich)*

Another mishap occurred on 8 June 1941 when X4031 was landing. The pilot, F/L Mrazek, escaped injuries. Mrazek would later become one of the six Czech DSO recipients in the RAF. Above, the undersurfaces are exposed showing the location of the roundels. *(Jiri Rajlich)*

A bad outcome for F/O Karel Vykoukal on board W3962 when he made a forced landing near Boscawen Rose Farm on 1 December 1941. He escaped unhurt. It was first thought that the aircraft was repairable but it was eventually re-categorised E a couple of weeks later.
(Jiri Rajlich)

The Mk. V was logically supplied to 313 and the first confrontations with the Luftwaffe arose in the spring of 1942. AA865 (see colour profile) was normally flown by Sgt Truhlar and was lost to enemy action with him at the controls on 10 April 1942.
(Jiri Rajlich)

Below, a presentation aircraft named 'GEO. S. PARKER' (the 'Parker Pen Spitfire'), AD384 was allocated to 313 Squadron on 21 October 1941. It was lost with its pilot, Sgt O. Kresta, the following 12 April (see operational losses) but Kresta survived to become a PoW.
(Andtew Thomas)

Above, three Mk. Vs of the squadron taxiing to carry out another operation during winter 41-42. W3969/RY-Y, AA765/RY-V and W3177/RY-W can be seen.
(Jiri Rajlich)
Left, EP644 in the summer of 1944. Note the Czech roundel on the front of the cockpit. This was unusual for 313.
(Andrew Thomas)
Below, AD361 under maintenance at Hornchurch in spring 1942.
(Jiri Rajlich)

Nice side view of AR549/RY-E during the summer of 1942. This Spitfire Mk. V served over a year with 313 before being passed on to the Polish 317 Squadron.

Two nice colour images extracted from vintage wartime footage taken in October 1942 when 313 was stationed at Hornchurch. The aircraft is Mk. V EP394.
(via Jiri Rajlich)

Top, Spitfire HF. IX ML148/RY-A with its full squadron markings. In 1945 this aircraft was usually flown by the CO, S/L Otmar Kučera. Above, MK965/RY-S. Below, a late arrival at the squadron, ML356, coded RY-O. Note the absence of any squadron or national markings on MK965 and ML356. The letter 'O' was common within 313 contrary to the regular RAF units. If all were HF. IX variants, not all were equipped with the pointed fin.

(Andrew Thomas)

Above, Spitfire HF. IX ML195/RY-F was usually flown by F/L František Masařík who was the A Flight Commander at the end of the war. Masařík was a pre-war Czechoslovakian air force pilot who had fled to France then to the UK. He served with various RAF squadrons before joining 313. This was the only Czech unit he would fly with which was contrary to many other Czechs who also served with either 310 or 312 or both.

Above, Spitfire HF. IX ML171 was the victim of an engine failure on take-off from Bradwell Bay on 7 January 1945. The pilot, Sgt Karel Stryk, escaped injuries. Stryk was a former Czechoslovakian member of the Army in France who switched to the RAF in September 1940 after his evacuation. Note the unusual location of the serial painted on the fuselage band.
(Jiri Rajlich)

Left, same cause, same consequence for NH250/RY-N on 20 June 1945 but this time flown by F/O Josef Stivar, a pre-war Czechoslovakian Air Force pilot. He served with the French before being evacuated to the UK. He completed one tour of operations with 310 (Czech) Squadron and another with 313.
(Jiri Rajlich)

Escort missions was the duty of No. 313 Squadron in 1945, each time with extra belly fuel tank. In the forefront, NH458/RY-B.
(Andrew Thomas)

Leconfield, August 1941, some members of the squadron pose for the camera. Sitting are F/L T. W. Gillen, F/O K. Vykoukal, S/L G. L. Sinclair DFC, P/O J. Muzika, F/O F. Fajtl, Sgt P. Brázda. Standing are Sgt J. Řezníček, Sgt V. Truhlar, F/Lt A. Walsham (Adjutant), P/O V. Jícha, F/O V. Hájek, F/O F. Zbořil, Sgt B. Dubec, Sgt J. Kučera, Sgt V. Foglar. *(Jiri Rajlich)*

Below, Plumetot in France, 28 June 1944. Far left, sitting on the wing is F/Sgt E. Smolka, standing on the wing is F/Sgt Charles Stojan, in the cockpit is S/Ldr A. Hochmal. In the front row, under Hochmal, and smiling at the bottle, is F/Sgt O. Špaček (5th from right), standing second from right is F/Lt R. Wood (with officer's cap and the bottle) and F/O John Pinny is on his left. *(Jiri Rajlich)*

Vaclav Jícha, Otmar Kučera and Josef Příhoda were all awarded the DFC on 6 October 1942. This photo was taken two weeks later during the investiture. All were pre-war Czechoslovakian air force pilots but only Kučera survived the war. Příhoda was shot down and killed by Fw190s on 6 March 1943 and Jícha was killed in a flying accident on 1 February 1945 when he was flying to Kinloss, Scotland, as a passenger in Anson NK945. The aircraft entered a snowstorm and crashed. The wreckage was only found on the 7th and it was thought that he may have survived but froze to death. *(Jiri Rajlich)*

Below, June 1941, the two non-Czech flight commanders with Frantisek Fajtl (on the right), a veteran of the Battle of France in May-June 1940 flying Moranes. Posted in May 1941 on the formation of 313, he would become a flight commander at the end of the year. He would later become the first Czech CO of a British-manned unit, 122 Squadron, and, later on, 313. After the war he returned to his country. The two flights were at that time under two experienced pilots. 'Jock' Gillen (left), formerly of 152, 247 and 403 Squadrons (the latter as a Flight Commander) would leave to take another flight commander position with 118 Squadron. He survived the war with the rank of Squadron Leader. In the middle is the Irishman 'Killy' Kilmartin who had become an ace during the Battle of France the previous year. He survived the war as a Wing Commander. *(Jiri Rajlich)*

The first three commanding officers of 313. Top left, Gordon Sinclair, a British pilot who would have a strong connection with the Czechs. A pre-war RAF pilot, he fought with 19 Squadron over Dunkirk where he made his first claims. In July 1940 he was posted as a Flight Commander to the newly-formed 310 Squadron, the first RAF Czechoslovakian unit to be formed, and was chosen to become the first OC of 313. He ended the war as a Wing Commander. He was replaced by Josef Jaške (top right), a pre-war fighter pilot in Czechoslovakia. Jaške fled to France and fought with the French flying Curtiss Hawks with which he made his first claims. Joining the RAF after the defeat of the French, he served with 312 (Czech) Squadron and eventually led a flight in 1941. In July 1941 he was posted to 313 with the aim to succeed Sinclair as OC (which happened in September 1941). No further operational postings followed after the end of his tour in December 1941. He returned to his country in 1945 and continued to serve in the new air force but was expelled in 1948 when the Communists took power. He fled once more and re-joined the RAF and served until 1968. Karel Mrazek took over the squadron in December 1941. He was also a pre-war army-cooperation and fighter pilot in Czechoslovakia and fled to France as early as May 1939 via Poland. He first enlisted in the French *Legion Etrangere* but when war broke out he was authorised to join the French Air Force. He flew a couple of sorties as a reconnaissance pilot with the French in June 1940 before fleeing to England where he joined the RAF. He participated in the Battle of Britain, with 310 (Czech) Squadron as a reserve pilot, then with Nos. 43 and 46 Squadrons. In 1941 he served with 257 (Burma) Squadron before joining 313 as a flight commander. He took over the Exeter Wing in June 1942 and led the unit until April 1943. He was one of the four Czech day fighter pilots to receive the DSO. Non-flying positions followed until the end of war. He returned to Czechoslovakia after the war and, as with Jaške, was expelled from the new air force in 1948 but, unlike his compatriot, decided to stay in the country.

Besides the commanding officers, 313 had some very experienced flight commanders, all pre-war Czechoslovakian military pilots, in its ranks. Top left, Václav Havek served with the French in Syria in 1940. Bohuslav Kimlička (top right) also served with the French but based in France. He also served with 310 during the war. František Masařík (below left) served with the French but did not fly operationally. With the RAF he served with 504 Squadron and later with 286. Karel Vykoukal (below right), like Masařík, never became operational with the French but participated in the Battle of Britain. He would be posted to 41 Squadron in April 1942 as a flight commander but was posted missing in mid-May and presumed killed. All the others survived the war. *(Jiri Rajlich)*

The first quarter of 1942 would become of the worst period for 313 as the squadron lost twelve pilots with all but one being killed (but taken prisoner). Not all were killed by enemy action however. Josef Valenta (top left), for example, had the dubious honour of becoming the first pilot to be killed, on 11 January, when he was returning in bad weather from an uneventful convoy patrol. The next month Frantisek Bonish was posted missing during another convoy patrol before Miroslav Zauf (top right) became the first squadron member to be lost over enemy territory during a Rhubarb operation.
However the first pilot to be killed by enemy action was Vladimír Michálek (left) who fell victim to Hauptmann Josef Priller of JG26 on 27 March.
(Jiri Rajlich)

In April it was Vaclav Truhlar's (top left) turn when, on the 10th, he became a PoW after combat against an Fw190 from JG26. Severely wounded, he was eventually repatriated to the UK in October 1943. František Pokorný (top right) was less lucky that day and was killed. Two days later Otakar Kresta crossed paths with Rolf Hermichen, another JG26 ace, and was shot down to spend the rest of the war in a PoW camp.*(Jiri Rajlich)*

In May 1942 313 lived through a very bad time as it lost many pilots. Karel Pavlík was shot down by Fw190s on 5 May during the same combat that F/L Stanislav Fejfar made his last claims. An ace with seven confirmed victories, two being shared and one more probable, he would survive a fortnight longer than Pavlík before falling victim to another ace, Hauptmann Josef Priller, who had shot down Vladimír Michálek in March. He wasn't the only pilot lost that day. Miroslav Birkovec (below left) was also killed while flying as Fejfar's wingman. To compensate the losses sustained during spring, some Czech pilots who were serving with other RAF units were urgently posted to 313. Jan Jeřábek (below left), one of the very few Czech pilots awarded the AFM during the war, was one of them. He arrived at the squadron in mid-June. He would, however, survive for only one month as he was shot down and killed by return fire from a Ju88 he was attacking.

(Jiri Rajlich)

The problem of flying personnel arose as early as 1940 but losses, the stress of an operational tour and the will to form a third fighter squadron led to a very tense situation in 1942 and forced the RAF to limit the operational usage of the Czech squadrons after Operation 'Jubilee' (Dieppe). Despite this, the personnel shortage persisted and became worse when some Czech fighter pilots resigned to serve with the Soviets in 1944. The Czechs tried to recruit fighter pilots from many sources, like Jaroslav Řehoř (top left), a former Czech groundcrew. He served with 313 from November 1944 onwards. Tomas Zrink (top right) was also former groundcrew (KIA 27.09.43). Bomber crew were even recruited. Karel Sláma (below), a former navigator who flew on Wellingtons with 311 Squadron, arrived at the squadron in March 1945. *(Jiri Rajlich)*

Despite all of these efforts, the number of Czech fighter pilots available remained below the normal requirements for three fighter squadrons. Other reinforcements had to be found and pilots coming from other air forces came to help. Robert A.C. Gaydos (left), for example, served between October 1943 and July 1944. He was born in the USA and the son of Slovakian emigrants. He first chose to enlist in the RAF, and later transferred to the USAAF, but still managed to serve with the Czech squadrons as he was posted to 312 in July 1944 and left in April 1945. *(Jiri Rajlich)*

The RAF and the RCAF provided about thirty pilots from mid-July 1943 to keep 313 operational. John Pinny (below) was among those who served the longest with the Czechs, being posted in during September 1943. He was killed on 1 February 1945 and was the last 313 pilot to lose his life.*(John Ellison)*

Summary of the operational activity
No. 313 (Czechoslovakian) Squadron

A/C types	First sortie	Last sortie	Total sorties	Tot Sub-type	Lost Ops	Lost Acc	A/C lost	Claims	V-1	Pilot †	PoWs	Eva.
Spitfire I	10.06.41	28.08.41	315	**315**	-	2	2	-	-	1	-	-
Spitfire II	15.08.41	02.12.41	477	**477**	-	-	-	-	-	-	-	-
Spitfire V	16.10.41	15.02.44	5,639	**5,960**	25	4	29	17.0	-	20	2	-
	12.07.44	30.09.44	321									
Spitfire VI	01.07.43	19.07.43	71	**71**	-	1	1	-	-	-	-	-
Spitfire VII	12.07.44	21.07.44	10	**10**	-	-	-	-	-	-	-	-
Spitfire IX	13.02.44	10.07.44	1,307	**2,137**	6	5	11	-	1	4	1	-
	02.10.44	12.05.45	830									
Others												
Tiger Moth	-	-	-	-	-	1	1	-	-	-	-	-
Other causes	-	-	-	-	-	-	-	-	-	-	-	-
Compilation	10.06.41	12.05.45	8,970	8,970	31	13	44	17.0	1.0	25	3	-

Main awards

DSO: -
DFC: 4
DFM: -

Points of interest :
Last fighter squadron to be formed with Czech pilots.

Unsolved mystery:

Statistics:
- Lost one aircraft every 289 sorties [Spitfire V: 238, Spitfire IX: 356]

BADGE
A hawk volant, wings elevated and addorsed.

MOTTO
JEDEN JESTRAB MNOHO VRAN ROZHAN
'One hawk chases away many crows'

Authority: King George VI, June 1945

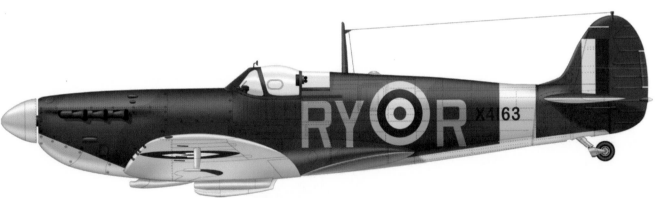

Supermarine Spitfire Mk.IA X4163, Caterick, June 1941.
Taken on charge on 9 August 1940, X4163 participated in the Battle of Britain with 54 Squadron before being passed on to 41 Squadron in February 1941, then to 452 (RAAF) in April and eventually to the 313 on 1 June 1941. Mainly used as a transition trainer, it was not assigned to a specific pilot. When it left the squadron at the end of October, it was to serve on as an advanced trainer at No. 53 OTU. This airframe has a long career and was SOC in May 1945.

Supermarine Spitfire Mk.VB W3962, Flying Officer Karel Vykoukal (Czech), Hornchurch, December 1941.
Taken on charge on 6 October 1941, W3962 was first issued to 313 (Czech) Squadron two weeks later where it became the regular mount of F/O Vykoukal. On 1 December he made a forced landing near Boscawen Rose Farm. It was first thought that it was repairable but the aircraft was eventually re-categorised Cat.E on 6 April 1942 (see p22).

Supermarine Spitfire Mk.VB AA865, Sergeant Vaclav Thruhlar (Czech), Hornchurch, 10 April 1942.
This Spitfire was taken on charge on 14 October 1941 and stored at No. 39 MU before being issued to the squadron on the 26TH. It was not allocated to any pilot and was lost in action on 10 April 1942 when it was shot down by Fw190s. The pilot, Sgt Truhlar, became a PoW. Above, two images showing the artwork 'Göbels'. On the right, lying on the beach with Luftwaffe personnel taking care of it. *(Jiri Rajlich)*

Supermarine Spitfire Mk.VB BL581, Flying Officer Karel Vykoukal (Czech), Hornchurch, March 1942.
BL581 was stored at No. 8 MU when taken on charge on 3 January 1942 and issued to the squadron on the 17th. It left as early as 30 March but was mostly flown by F/L Vykoukal while with 313. It later served with Nos. 152 and118 Squadrons and was eventually lost on 11 April 1944.

Supermarine Spitfire Mk.VB BL973, F/L Stanislav Fejfar (Czech), Fairlop, 17 May 1942.
Taken on charge on 28 February 1942, its was issued to the Squadron at the end of March where it became the personal mount of Flight Lieutenant Fejfar who would
be shot down and killed in this aircraft on 17 May.

Supermarine Spitfire HF.IX, Bradwell Bay (UK), January 1945.
This Spitfire was taken on RAF charge on 28 March 1944. Two months later it was issued to 74 Squadron before passing to 312 (Czech) Squadron on 8 July and then
313 on 5 October. As with all Spitfire IXs of this unit, it was not allocated to any pilot. It fell victim to an engine failure on take off from Bradwell Bay on 7 January 1945
but the pilot, Sgt Karel Stryk, escaped injury. The camouflage and markings were standard but the small size of the serial painted on the fuselage band is unusual.
ML171 was repaired to continue its career with the RAF after the war.

Supermarine Spitfire HF.IX, Manston (UK), Spring 1945.
ML195 was taken on charge on 18 April 1944. As with ML171, it was issued to 74 Squadron but on 19 May. It then passed to 312 (Czech) Squadron and stayed there
from 10 July to the 28th when it returned to 74. It was issued to 313 on 10 May 1945 and survived the war. It remained with the RAF until to be sold to Vickers-
Armstrong in November 1949.

SQUADRONS!
No.3

USN AIRCRAFT
1922-1962

Vol. 2:
Designation Letter

*RAF, DOMINION & ALLIED SQUADRONS
AT WAR:
STUDY, HISTORY AND STATISTICS*

No.137 Squadron
1941 - 1945

COMPILED BY

Fighter Leaders
of the RAF, RAAF, RCAF, RNZAF & SAAF in WW2

Volume I

Phil H. Listemann

Fighter Leaders
of the RAF, RAAF, RCAF, RNZAF & SAAF in WW2

Volume II

Phil H. Listemann

SQUADRONS!
No.10

The North American
Mustang Mk. IV
in Western Europe

www.RAF-IN-COMBAT.com

- USN Aircraft 1922-1962 -
- Squadrons! -
- RAF, Dominion and Allied squadrons at War -
- Allied Wings -
- Famous squadrons of WW2 -
- Fighter Leaders -

*RAF, DOMINION & ALLIED SQUADRONS
AT WAR:
STUDY, HISTORY AND STATISTICS*

Famous Commonwealth Squadrons of WW2

No.453 (R.A.A.F) Squadron
1941-1945
Buffalo, Spitfire

No.131 (County of Kent) Squadron
1941 - 1945

COMPILED BY

LISTEMANN

PHIL H. LISTEMANN

SQUADRONS!
No.9

The Forgotten
Fighters

ALLIED WINGS

No.18
The Supermarine SPITFIRE
F.24

Phil H. Listemann

Phil H. Listemann

21801315R00026

Printed in Poland
by Amazon Fulfillment
Poland Sp. z o.o., Wrocław